W9-DIH-875

INFORMATION EXPLORER JUNIOR

Find New Words with Dictionaries

by Ann Truesdell

CHERRY LAKE PUBLISHING · ANN ARBOR, MICHIGAN

A NOTE TO PARENTS AND TEACHERS: Please remind your children how to stay safe online before they do the activities in this book.

A NOTE TO KIDS: Always remember your safety comes first!

CHERRY LAKE Publishing

Published in the United States of America
by Cherry Lake Publishing
Ann Arbor, Michigan
www.cherrylakepublishing.com

Content Adviser: Gail Dickinson, PhD, Associate Professor, Old Dominion University

Book design and illustration: The Design Lab

Photo credits: Cover, ©iStockphoto.com/Imagesbybarbara; page 5, ©Dmitriy
Shironosov/Shutterstock, Inc.; page 6, ©Terrance Emerson/Dreamstime.com; page
13, ©iStockphoto.com/SilviaJansen; page 19, ©Sebastian Czapnik/Dreamstime.com;
page 21, ©LUCARELLI TEMISTOCLE/Shutterstock, Inc.

Library of Congress Cataloging-in-Publication Data
Truesdell, Ann.
  Find new words with dictionaries / by Ann Truesdell.
      p. cm.—(Information explorer junior)
  Includes bibliographical references and index.
  ISBN 978-1-61080-368-7 (lib. bdg.)—ISBN 978-1-61080-377-9 (e-book)—
ISBN 978-1-61080-393-9 (pbk.)
1. English language—Dictionaries—Juvenile literature. 2. Encyclopedias and
dictionaries—Juvenile literature. I. Title.
  PE1611.T78 2012
  423—dc23   2011034503

Cherry Lake Publishing would like to acknowledge
the work of The Partnership for 21st Century Skills.
Please visit www.21stcenturyskills.org for more information.

Printed in the United States of America
Corporate Graphics Inc.
January 2012
CLSP10

Table of Contents

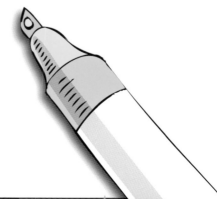

CHAPTER ONE

A World of Words

Did you know that the English language is made up of hundreds of thousands of words? It's true! So what do you do if you hear or read a word that you do not know? Look it up in a **dictionary**! A dictionary is a **resource** that can be a book or an online Web site. It is all about words. It gives you the meaning of words. A dictionary shows you the correct spellings, too. It also tells you how to **pronounce** words, or say them out loud.

dictionary (DIK-shuh-ner-ee)

A dictionary tells you what a word means, gives you the correct spelling, and tells you how to pronounce the word.

Most libraries have many kinds of dictionaries available for people to use.

There are many different kinds of dictionaries. Some are for adults, while others are for children. Some dictionaries have pictures to help you understand what the words mean. Turn the page and find out more about printed and online dictionaries!

CHAPTER TWO

Tips for Using a Printed Dictionary

Some dictionaries have information about thousands of different words.

First, let's learn to use a dictionary that is a book. This is known as a printed dictionary.

You need to understand **alphabetical order** to use a printed dictionary. The words are listed starting with the "A" words. Then come the "B" words. The words continue in order and end with the "Z" words.

octopus

queen

ABCDEFGHIJKLMNOPQRSTUVWXYZ

In a dictionary, which word comes first, "octopus" or "queen"? If you are unsure, look at the alphabet above.

All of the words are in alphabetical order again within each letter section! Words are spelled using letters in a special order. Look at the order of the letters in each word. For example, look at the B section of the dictionary. "Baboon" comes before "baby." That's because of the alphabetical order of each letter in each word.

baboon

baby

The first three letters of "baboon" and "baby" are the same. Look at the fourth letter to decide which word is first in a dictionary.

ace-ape

ace

ape

apple-assist

apple-

assist-

Use the guide words to quickly find what you're looking for.

Printed dictionaries have **guide words** at the top of each page. These help you find your word. Guide words tell you the first word and the last word on that page. For example, one page might show all the words between "ace" and "ape." Ask yourself these questions: Does my word fit between these two guide words? Does my word come before the first guide word? Does it come after the second guide word?

Activity

You must know
alphabetical order to
use a printed dictionary.
Let's practice! First, see if you can arrange the
following words in alphabetical order:

bear   bed   banjo   bead   bake

Now let's practice using guide words. Pretend you
are looking in a printed dictionary for the word
"berry." The guide words at the top of the page
you turn to are "bear" and "bed." Will your word
be on this page? Will it be on a page before this
one? Will it be on a page after this one?

(Answer: bake, banjo, bead, bear, bed)

You are correct if you said that it would be on a page after this page. "Bed" is the second guide word. "Berry" comes after "bed" in alphabetical order. So "berry" will not be on this page. It will be on a page after this one. You will have to turn the page and check out the next set of guide words. Keep looking until you find which guide words are a match. Then you can scan the page until you see your word!

bear – bed

bee – box

berry

To get a copy of this activity, visit www.cherrylakepublishing.com/activities.

CHAPTER THREE

Get On with Your Online Search!

Do your best to spell your word the correct way.

Now let's learn how to use an online dictionary. Many online dictionaries let you search for your word just by typing it in. But what if you do not know how to spell the word? Take your best guess. The online dictionary takes you to the word's **entry** if you spell it right. If you do not spell it right, that's OK. The dictionary will probably give you a list of words that are close to what you typed in. Choose the correct spelling. The dictionary will take you to the word you were looking for.

Online dictionaries are great tools for helping with homework.

To get a copy of this activity, visit www.cherrylakepublishing.com/activities.

Activity

There are many dictionaries on the Internet. A children's dictionary is a good choice for students. You can find one by using a **search engine** page. A search engine is a computer program that helps you find information you are looking for. Some good search engines for kids are:

www.boolify.org
http://kids.yahoo.com
http://kidsclick.org

Many search engines even search dictionaries for you! Type in the word "define" and then type your word after it into a search engine. Can you find an online dictionary that is meant just for kids? Does your library Web site have any links to online dictionaries?

CHAPTER FOUR

Unlocking the Secrets of a Dictionary Entry

Reading dictionary entries is an important skill.

An entry looks the same in online and printed dictionaries. Let's learn how to read a dictionary entry.

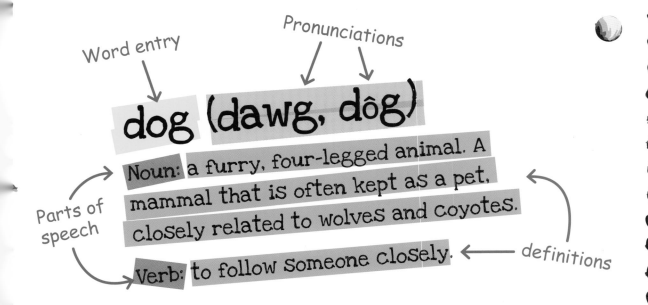

Word entry

Pronunciations

dog (dawg, dôg)

Parts of speech

Noun: a furry, four-legged animal. A mammal that is often kept as a pet, closely related to wolves and coyotes.

Verb: to follow someone closely.

definitions

Let's look up the word "dog." In the entry, the word "dog" is listed in bolder or bigger letters. This lets you know that you are looking at the correct entry. Do you see the next bolder or larger word below yours? That is the start of an entry for a different word.

This entry includes a section that shows you how to pronounce the word. It might say that "dog" is pronounced "dawg." You might be able to hear your word being said out loud. You can sometimes click on a button to hear it. This can be very helpful!

Each entry tells you the **definition** of your word, or what the word means. There can be many definitions for each word. The dictionary points out the **part of speech** for each definition. The part of speech tells you what kind of word it is and how it is used in a sentence. For example, the word "dog" is both a noun and a verb! As a noun, it means the animal. The verb "dog" means to follow someone very closely. A dictionary helps you understand the different meanings.

"Dog" as a noun.

A dictionary also shows the spellings of words used in different ways. Sometimes you want to make a word **plural**. That means you have more than one of that item. The plural of "dog" is "dogs." You add an "s" to the end of the word. Now you are talking about more than one dog. Not all plural words add "s" to the end. Some plural words add "es" to the end. One dish, two dishes. A dictionary tells you the right way to do this for each word.

dishes

dish

A dictionary tells you how to make a word plural.

Some dictionaries include more information than others do.

Most dictionaries also include other words that are related to the entry. These words may help you better understand a word. The dictionary may also put the word in a sentence. That way, you can see how it is used. Some dictionaries even include pictures.

Activity

Find a printed or online dictionary. Look up the following words. What do they mean? Do they have more than one meaning? Do the definitions show different parts of speech?

	part of speech	definition
address		
lean		
stand		
run		
eye		
coat		
iron		
bow		
trunk		

STOP
DON'T WRITE IN THIS BOOK!

Did you notice that many words have more than one meaning? The dictionary is filled with words that you may not know! You will learn something every time you use the dictionary.

What words will you learn next?

Glossary

alphabetical order (al-fah-BET-uh-kul OR-dur) an A-to-Z order, or listing things in the order of the alphabet

definition (def-uh-NISH-uhn) an explanation of the meaning of a word

dictionary (DIK-shuh-ner-ee) a resource that lists words in alphabetical order and explains what they mean, how to pronounce them, and what part of speech they are

entry (EN-tree) a word that is listed in a dictionary

guide words (GIDE WORDZ) words that are found at the top of each page in a printed dictionary, which show the first and last words on that page

part of speech (PART UHV SPEECH) the form of a word, such as noun, verb, adjective, or adverb

plural (PLOOR-uhl) the form of a word used for two or more of something

pronounce (pruh-NOUNTS) to say words out loud

resource (REE-sorss) something you can go to for help, such as a dictionary or encyclopedia

search engine (SURCH EN-juhn) a computer program that helps you find words or information you request

Find Out More

BOOKS

DK Merriam-Webster Children's Dictionary. New York: Dorling
    Kindersley Publishing, 2008.

Scholastic Children's Dictionary. New York: Scholastic
    Reference, 2011.

WEB SITES

**Enchanted Learning—Word Definition
and Dictionary Activities**
www.enchantedlearning.com/dictionary
A fun Web site that tests your dictionary skills with scavenger
hunts and lets you print your own activity books on dozens
of subjects.

Wordsmyth
www.wordsmyth.net
Check out this great online dictionary that has
audio pronunciations, illustrations and
cartoons, make-your-own quizzes,
and lots more.

Index

About the Author

Ann Truesdell is a school library media specialist and teacher in Michigan. She and her husband, Mike, love traveling and spending time with their children, James and Charlotte.